MAZES FOR KIDS
Ages 4 to 8

Fun and challenging maze puzzles for kids' entertainment
(learning activities workbook)

Introduction

Maze puzzles are a great way of boosting your kids' concentration and patience. Solving maze puzzles also helps with their memory, coordination and   problem solving skills.

They can also help develop your kids' muscle tone and improve their writing skills, even without writing any letters.

As maze puzzles are quite ageless, anyone can try to solve them, so it can be a fun family activity.

Let's have fun discovering the paths hidden in the drawings in these pages! Are you ready?

My First Car

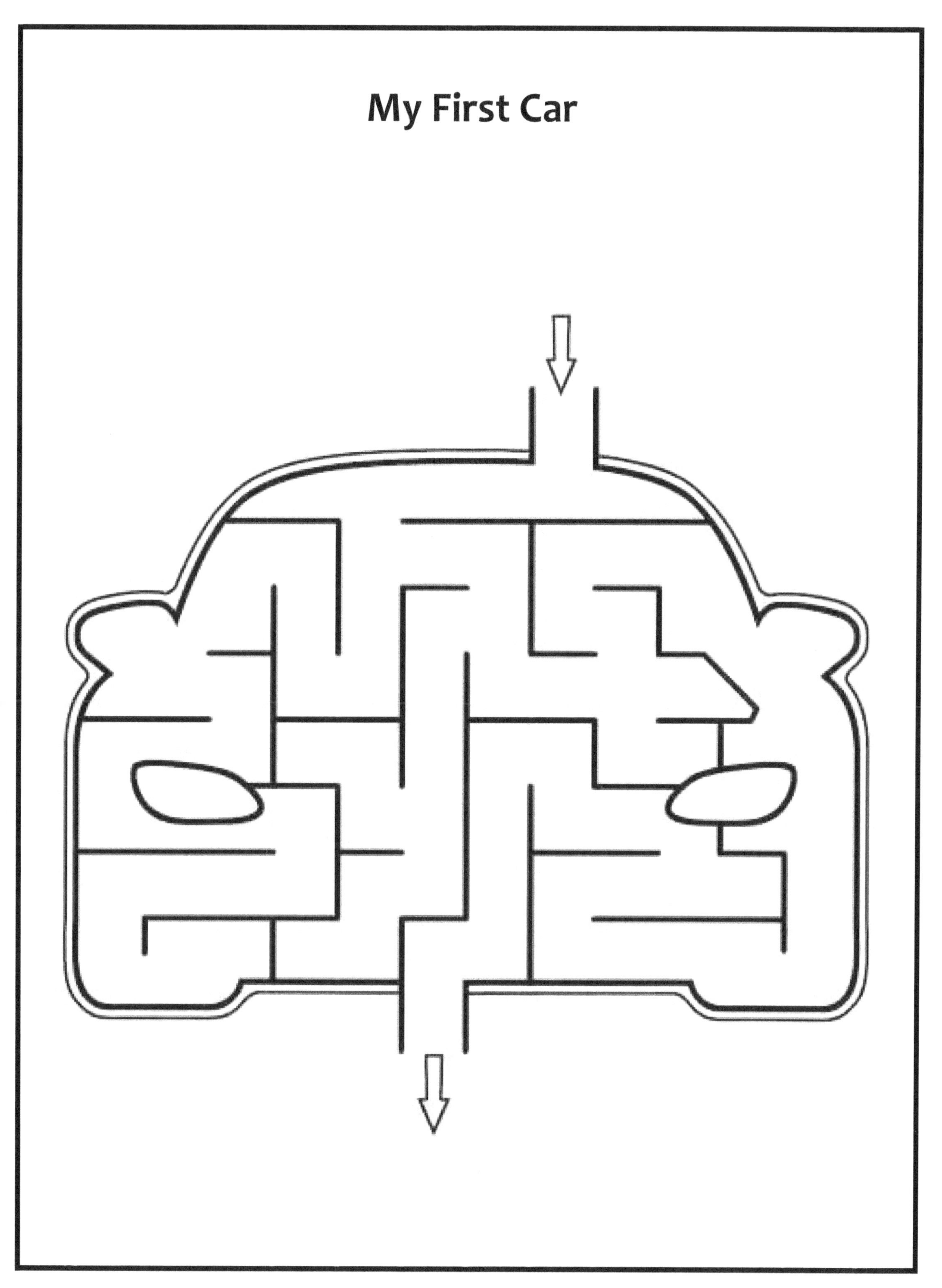

Neverending Story

My Big Friend

Let's Fly!

Beautiful Ballerina

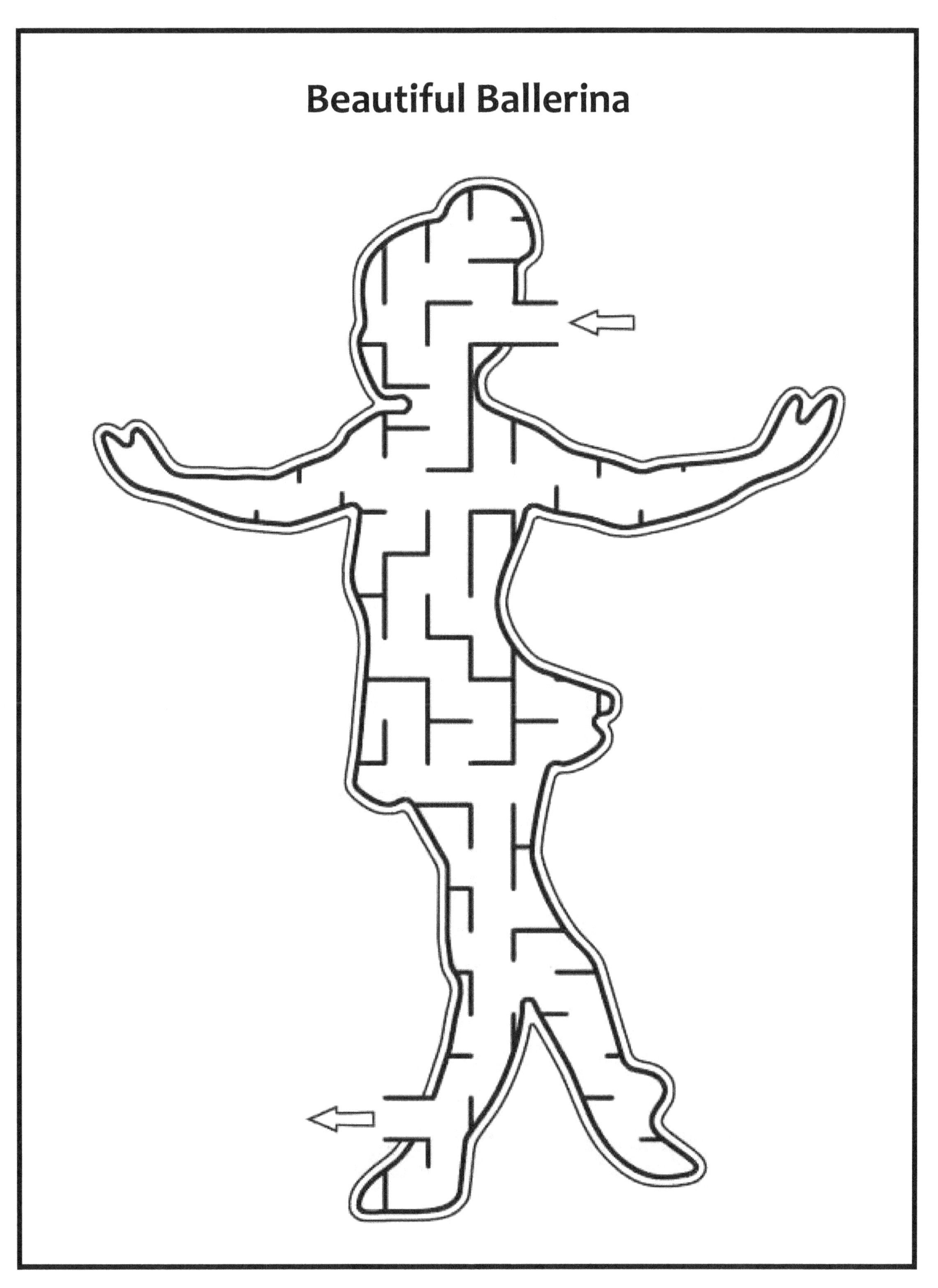

The Enchanted Castle

Light It Up!

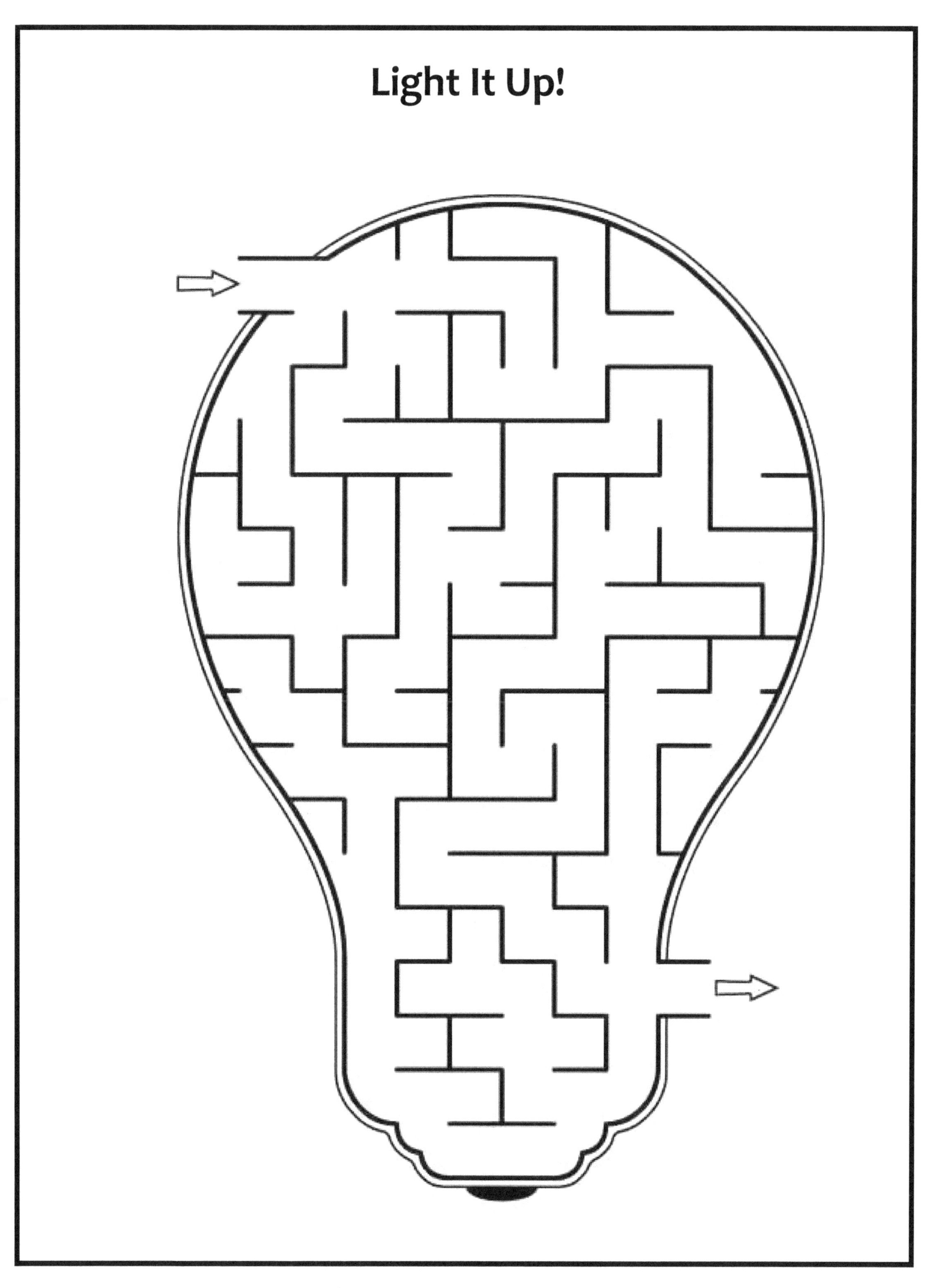

Baby Elephant

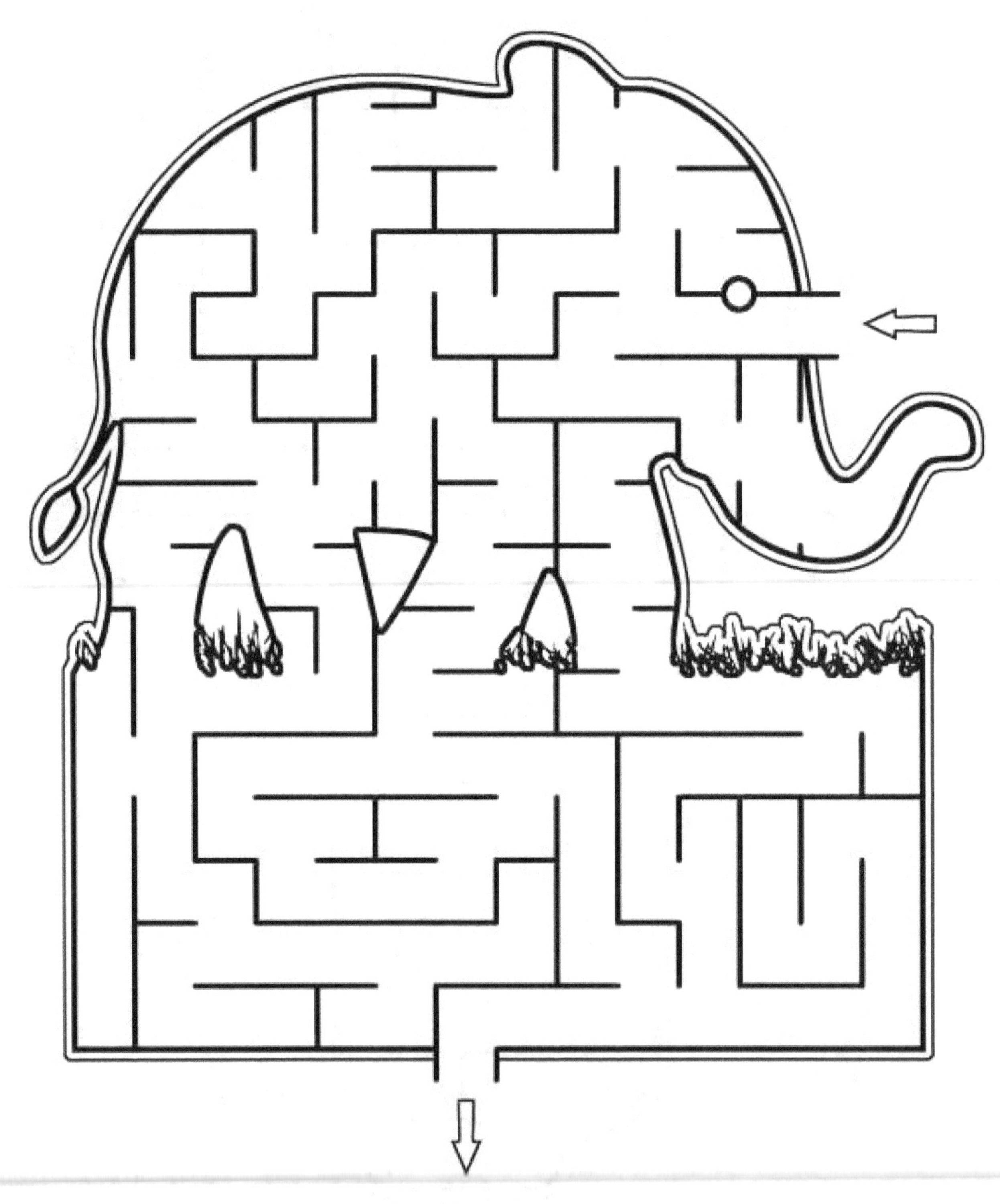

The Roman Colosseum

Do You Like Music?

Howdy!

Moon, Here We Go!

Nice Glasses

My Polar Friend

Nice Smile, T-Rex!

Little Pianist

Welcome to India

Dubai Skyline

Ready for the Adventure?

Are There any Fish Down There?

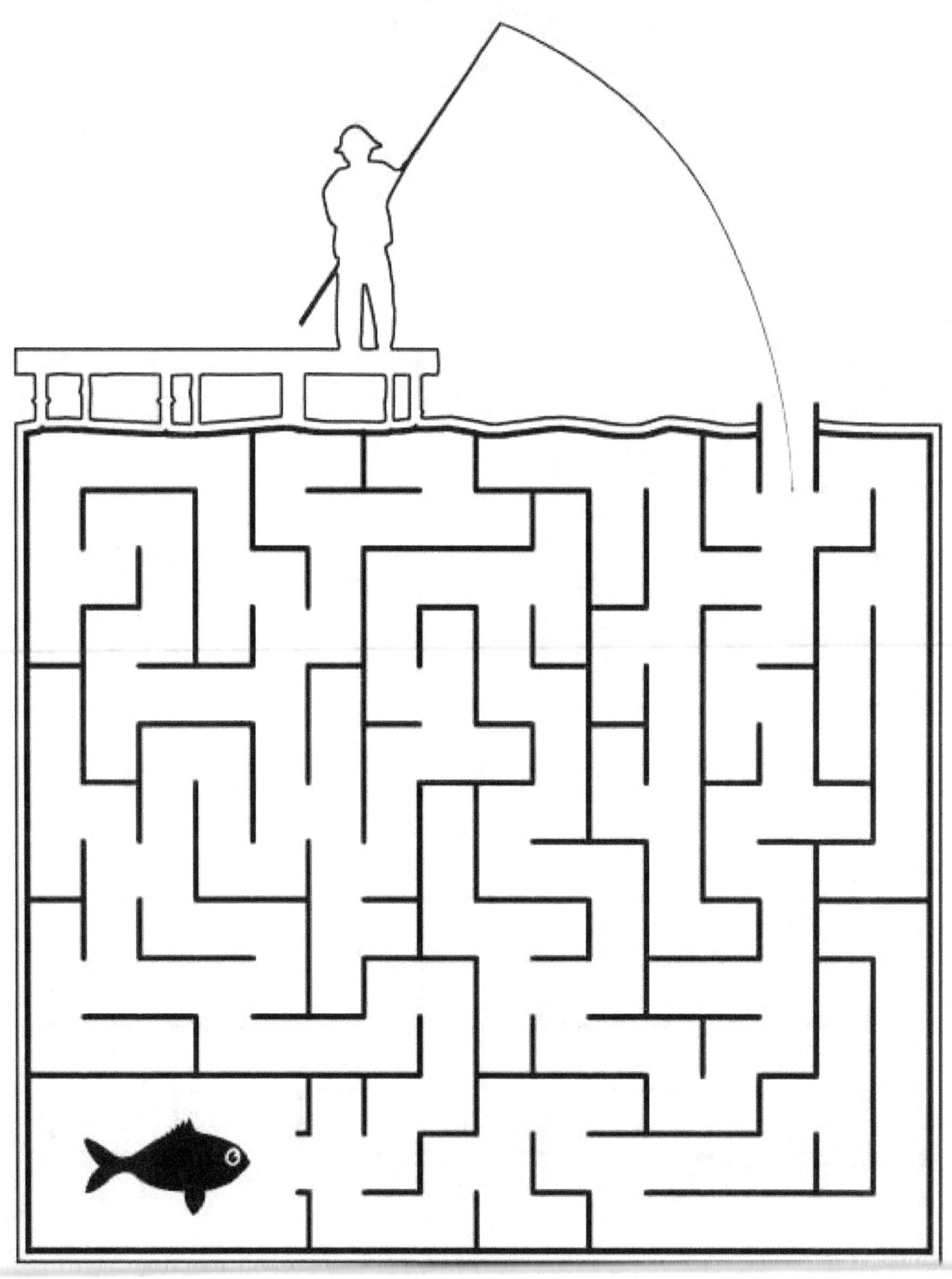

Easter Bunny

Up High in the Sky

Seal the Deal!

My Backyard Tree

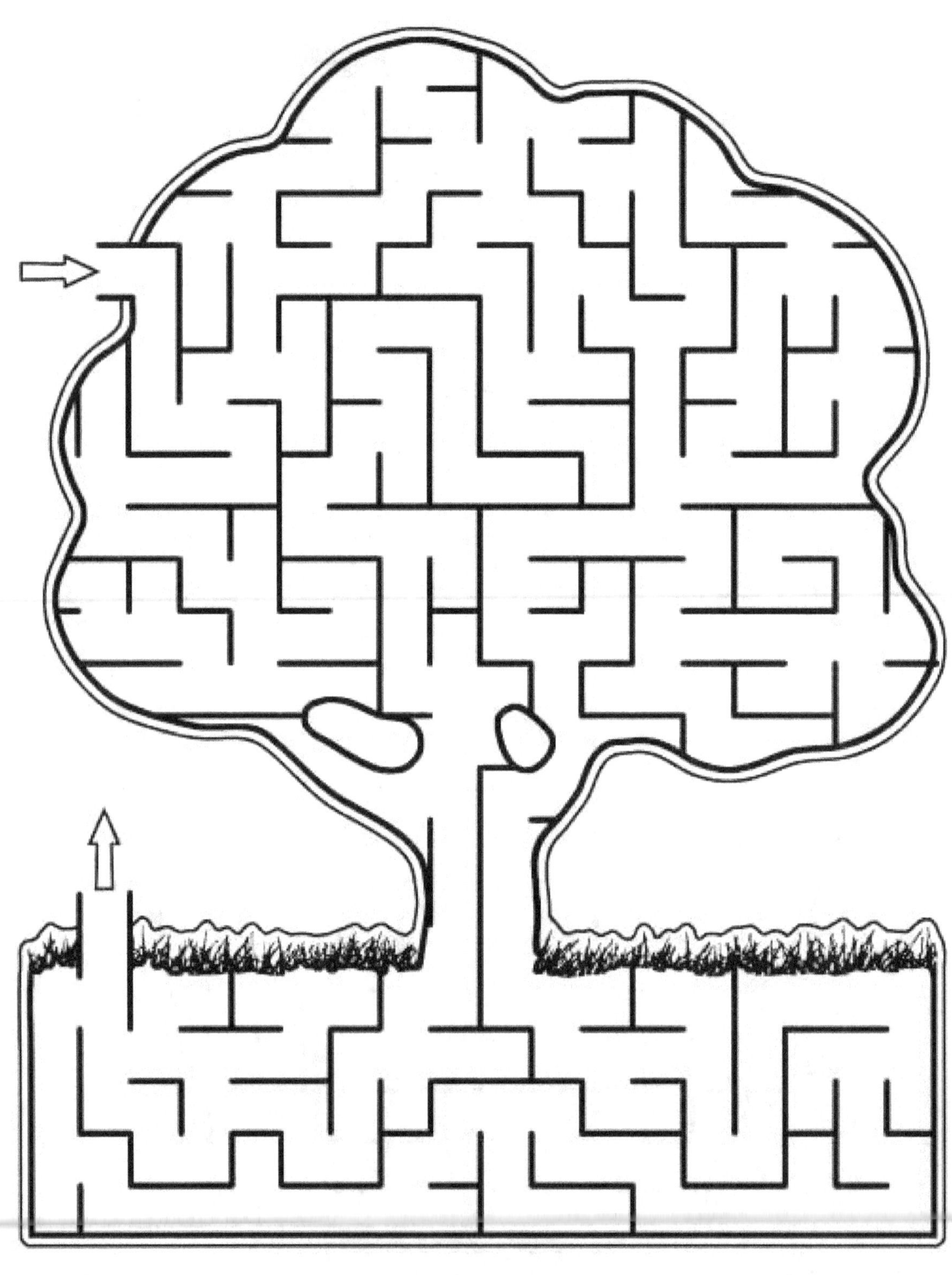

Gymnastics

Ahoy, Captain!

Paris, the City of Love

Morning Bike Ride

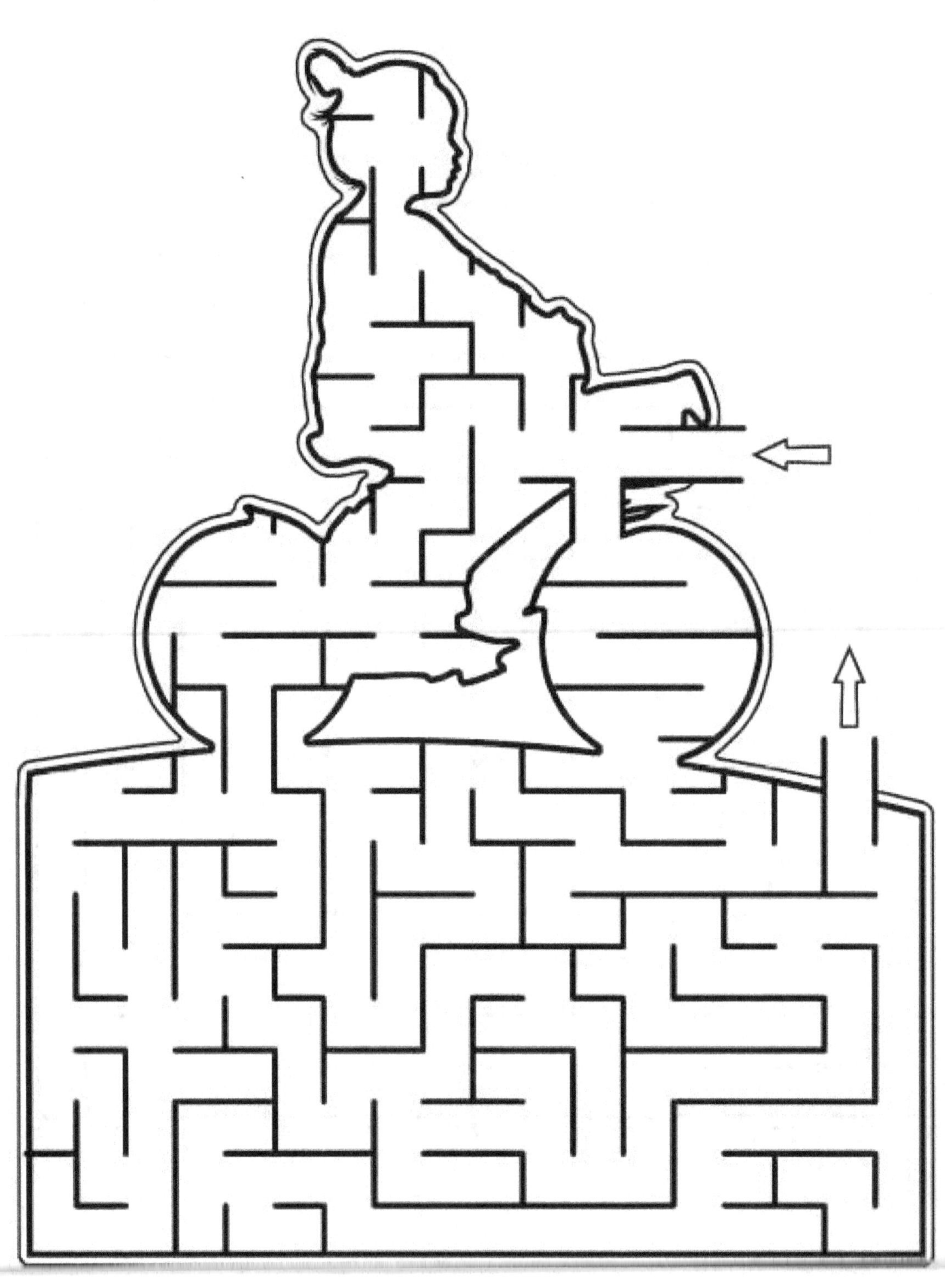

Do You Have Good Aim?

Skiing Down the Hill

Fresh Water

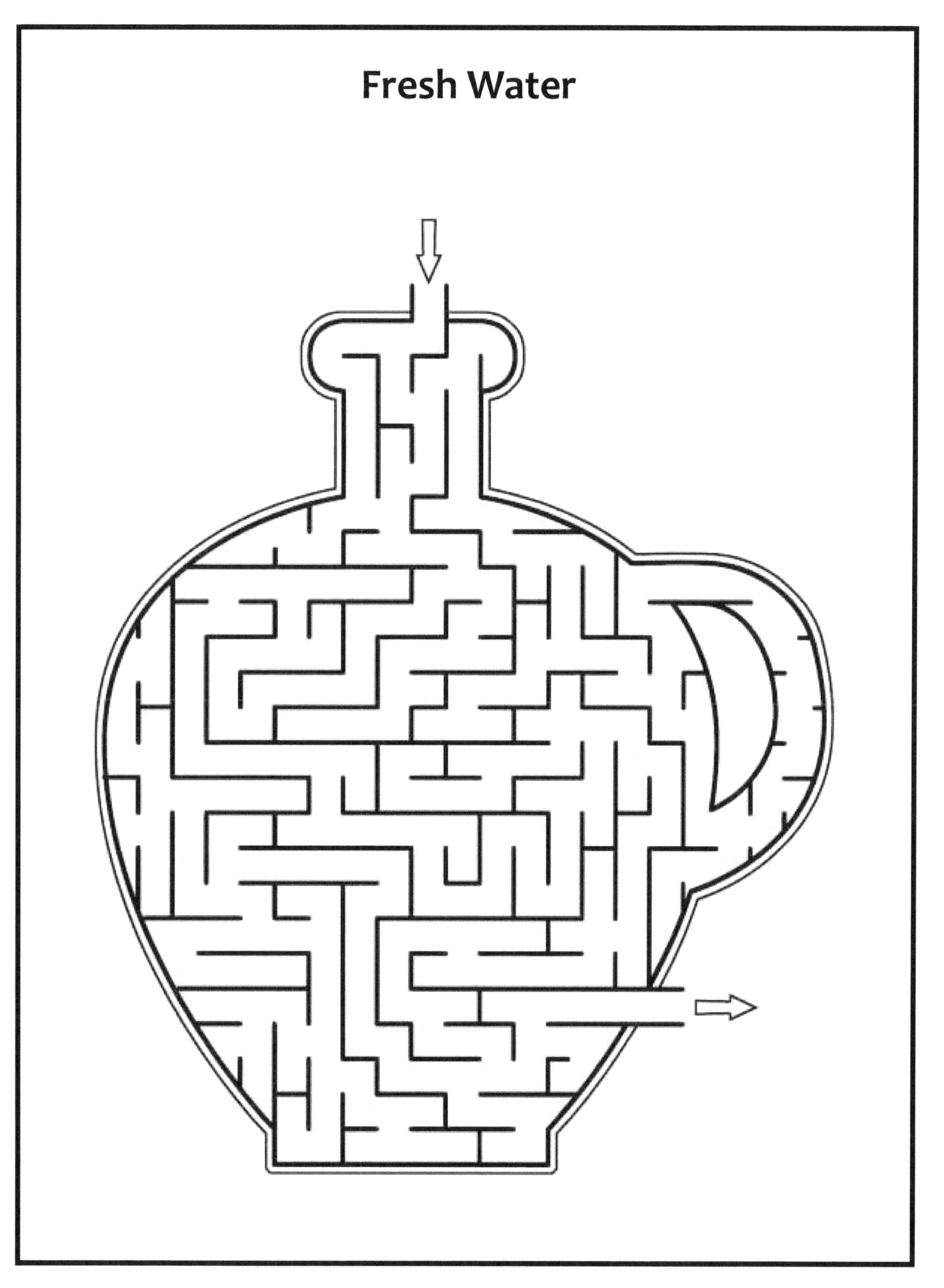

My Jurassic Friend

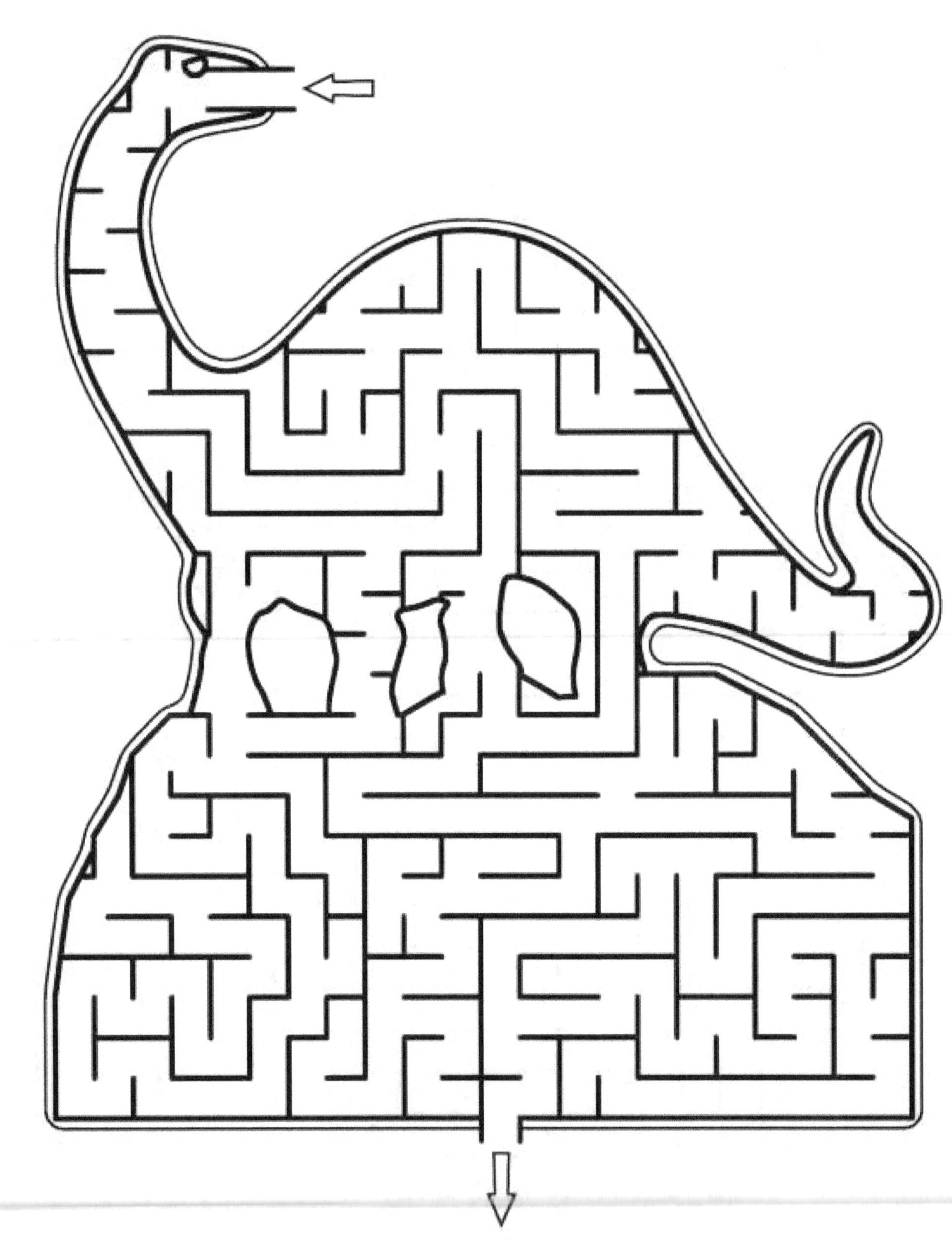

Boo!

What's Inside You?

Karate Kids

Polar Express

A Friendly Rhino

New York, New York

Tea Time in London

Deep Blue Sea

King of the Jungle

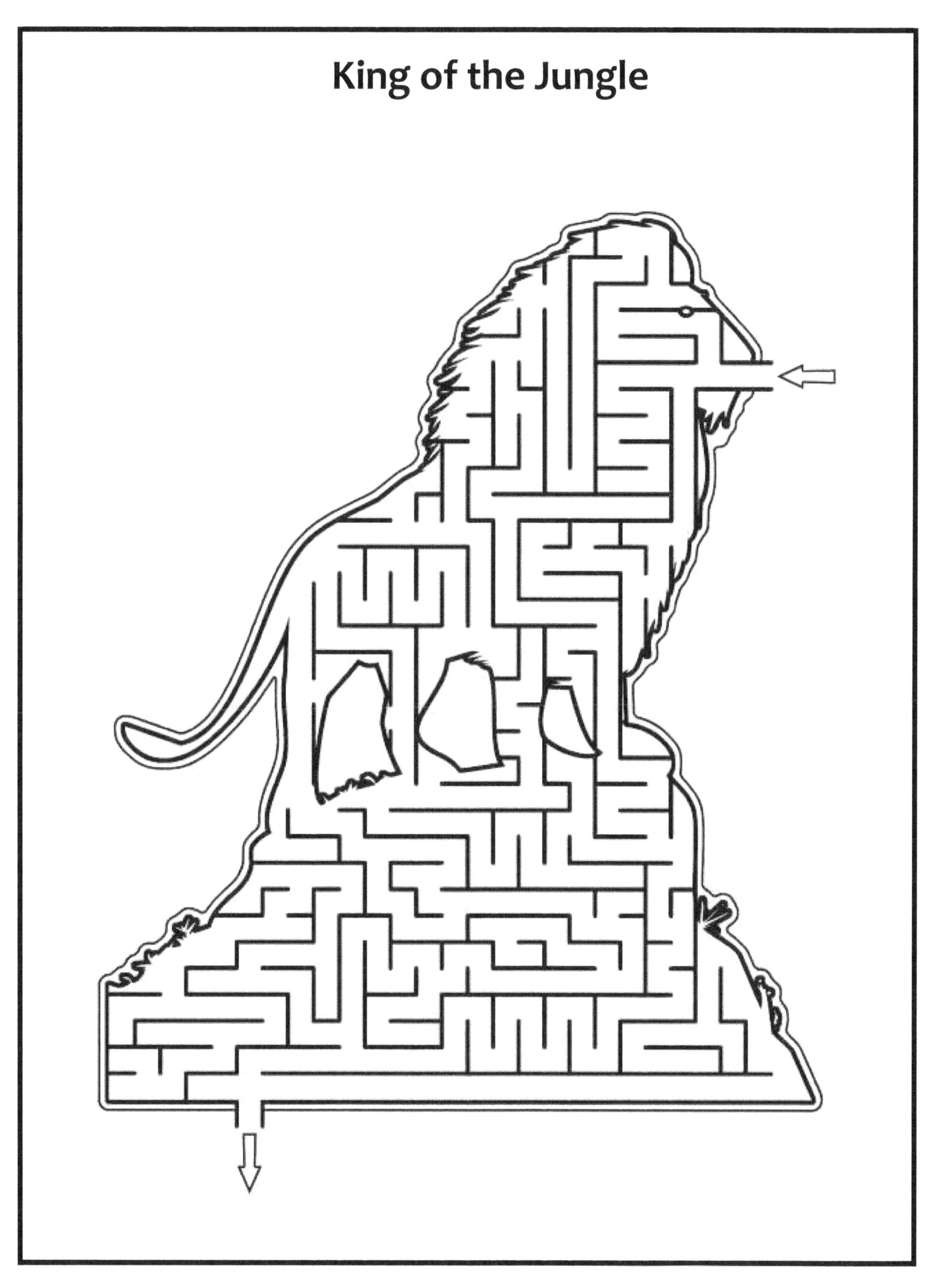

Are You Thirsty?

Cool Bike!

My Lovely Pet

Yeehaw!

Dance, Dance, Dance...

Ancient Egypt

Careful with the Ship!

Night at the Sydney Opera House

Are There any Diamonds Down There?

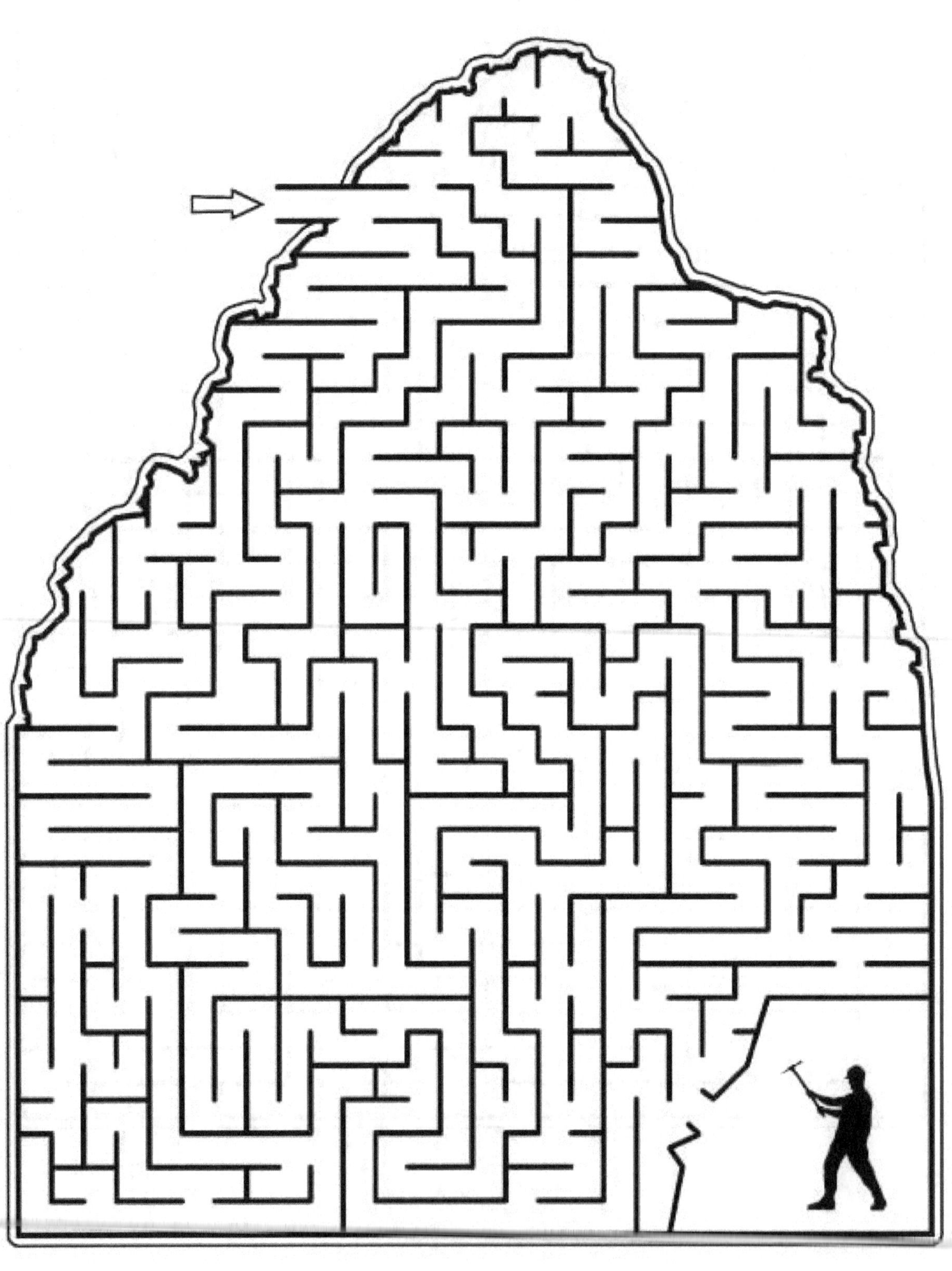

Conclusions

Congratulations on making it to the end of this Mazes book. I hope you and your kids had a great time solving these puzzles.

Now you can try to solve them backwards and if you get stuck, here's a tip: you can pretend that you are inside the maze with your hand touching the wall, doesn't matter if left or right, that way you will eventually find the right path.

Finally, if you found this book useful and fun, a positive review on Amazon is always appreciated!